How BIG WERE DINOSAURS?

How BIG WERE DINOSAURS?

LITA JUDGE

ROARING BROOK PRESS
NEW YORK

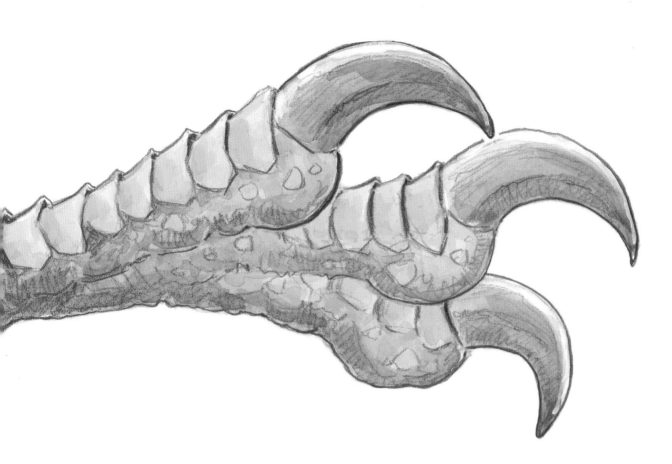

Stalking, stomping, running, crushing.

When we think of dinosaurs we think of huge **MONSTERS**. But how big were dinosaurs **REALLY**?

MICRORAPTOR was a deadly hunter, but he would barely be able to look a modern-day chicken in the eye.

The truth is, dinosaurs came
in all shapes and sizes.

PROTOCERATOPS had very large skulls and heavy beaks for ripping tough plants. They were strong and built for defense, but no bigger than a baby rhinoceros.

And honestly, with a name like **LEAELLYNASAURA,**
you'd think these dinosaurs were tree-eating giants.

But they stood only two feet tall. They lived through the cold, dark winters near the South Pole, where emperor penguins live today.

Even **VELOCIRAPTOR,** a dinosaur that
fills our imagination with its flesh-ripping claws and
powerful jaws, was only the size of a dog.

STRUTHIOMIMUS were the perfect size for going to the races. With slender legs and long tails they were built like a very light horse, and ran just as fast—up to 35 miles an hour!

ANKYLOSAURUS was a little taller than an SUV but weighed four times as much. Built to withstand attack, they were covered in armored plates and sharp spikes. And they had a great bony club for a tail. Imagine being stuck in a traffic jam with a cranky *Ankylosaurus*!

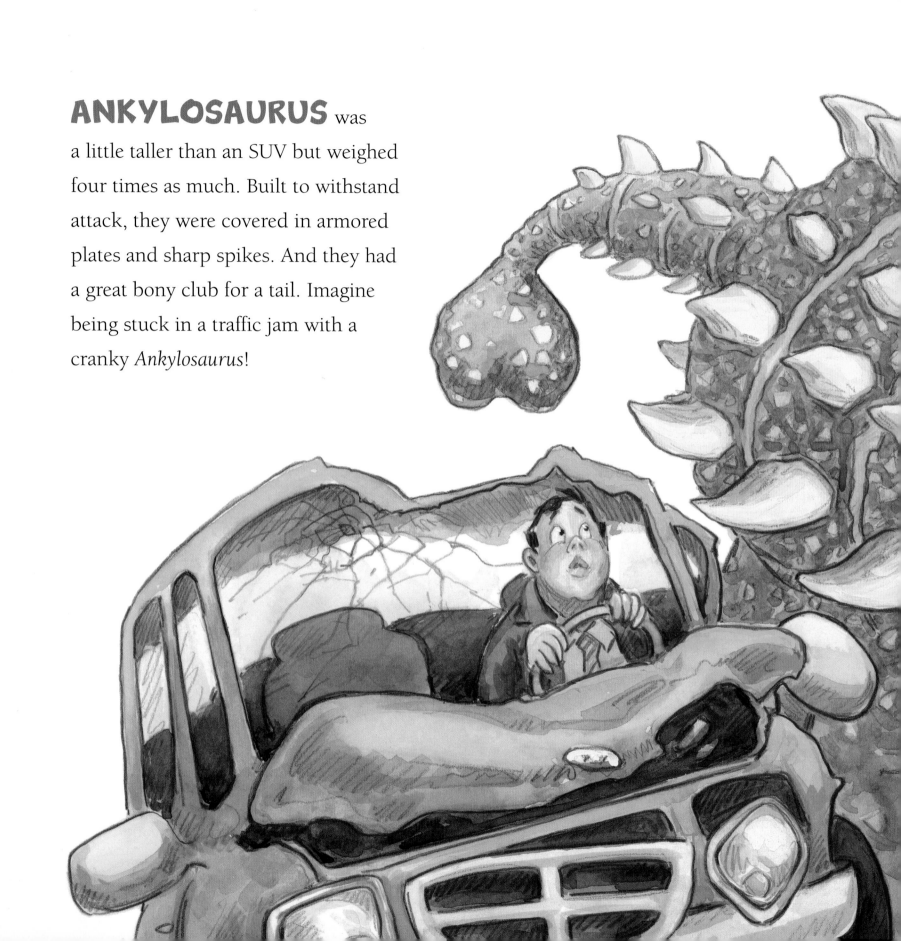

STEGOSAURUS

weighed as much as three cows, but with bony plates on his back that could be up to 3 feet long, he looked much bigger. Bigger isn't always smarter—this giant plant-eater only had a brain the size of a walnut.

Like a giant unicorn, **TSINTAOSAURUS** had a strange spike growing out of its skull. We don't know what this spike was used for, but with a dinosaur-sized appetite and hundreds of teeth, he could have gobbled your garden in a few quick bites.

TOROSAURUS had a 10-foot skull and horns that grew as tall as a first grader. You wouldn't want to make this dinosaur do something he didn't want to do.

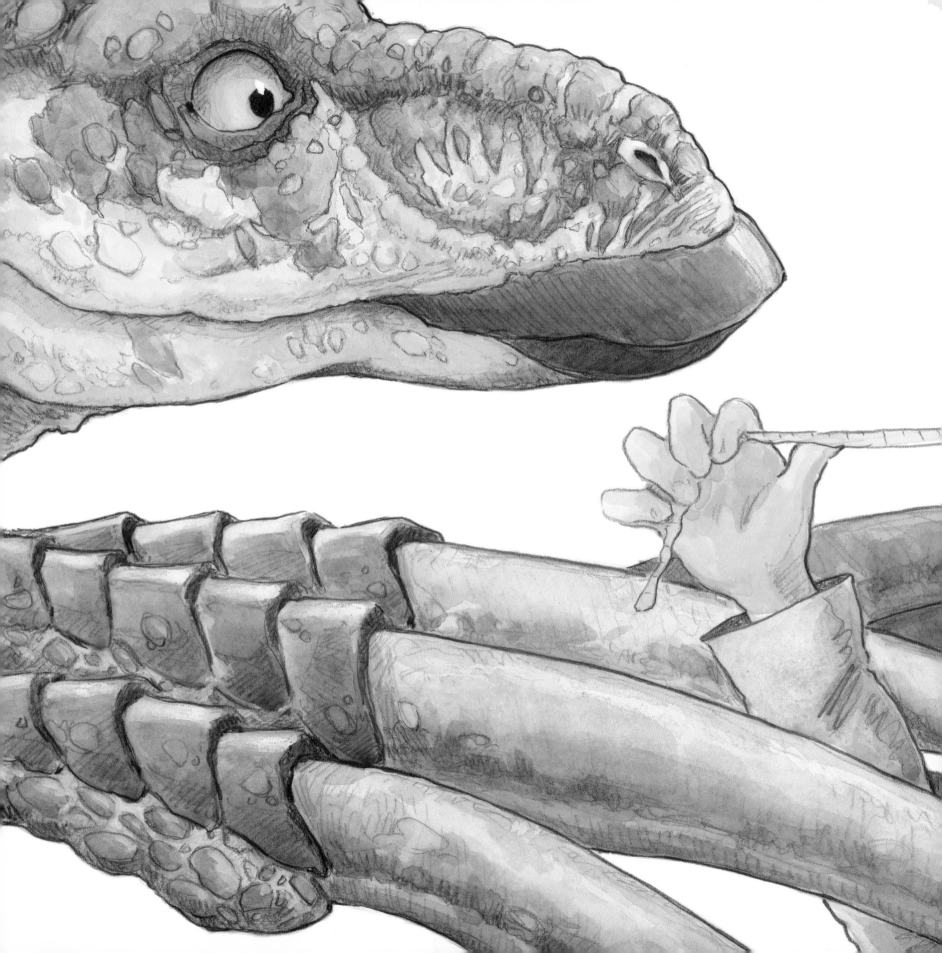

THERIZINOSAURUS had claws that grew up to 36 inches, longer than a man's arm. But don't worry—these plant-eaters most likely used their claws to strip bark off trees and pull down branches.

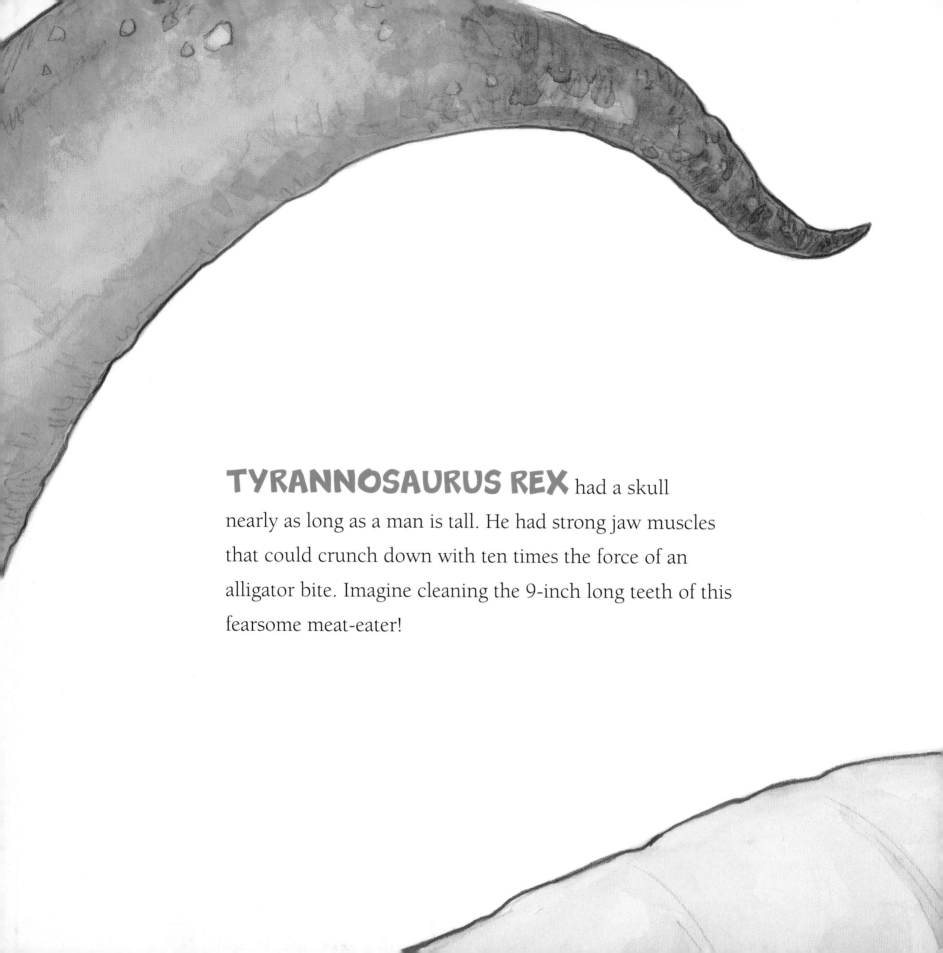

TYRANNOSAURUS REX had a skull nearly as long as a man is tall. He had strong jaw muscles that could crunch down with ten times the force of an alligator bite. Imagine cleaning the 9-inch long teeth of this fearsome meat-eater!

But even the fierce *Tyrannosaurus rex*
was no match for the biggest, most
ENORMOUS,
COLOSSAL
GIANT of them all . . .

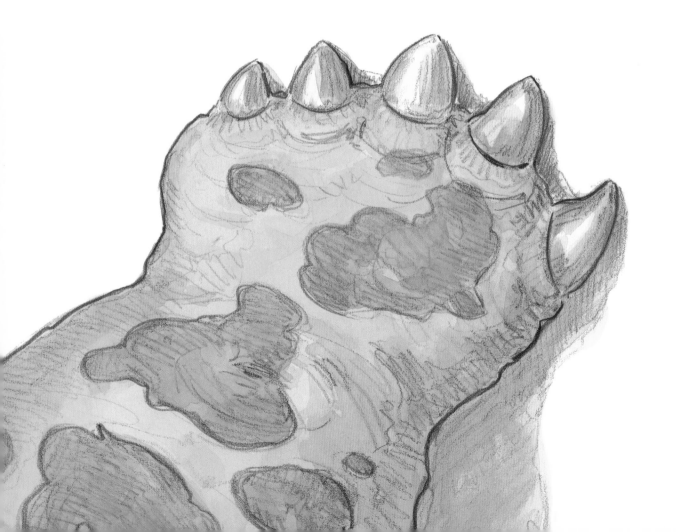

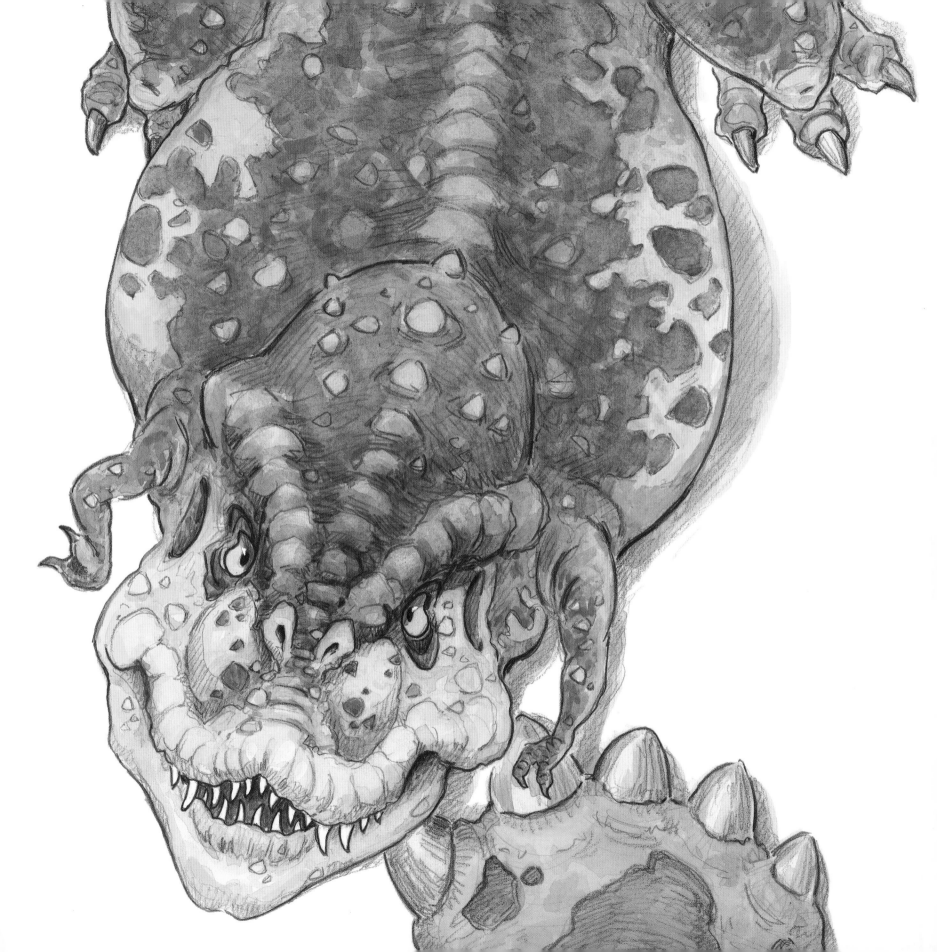

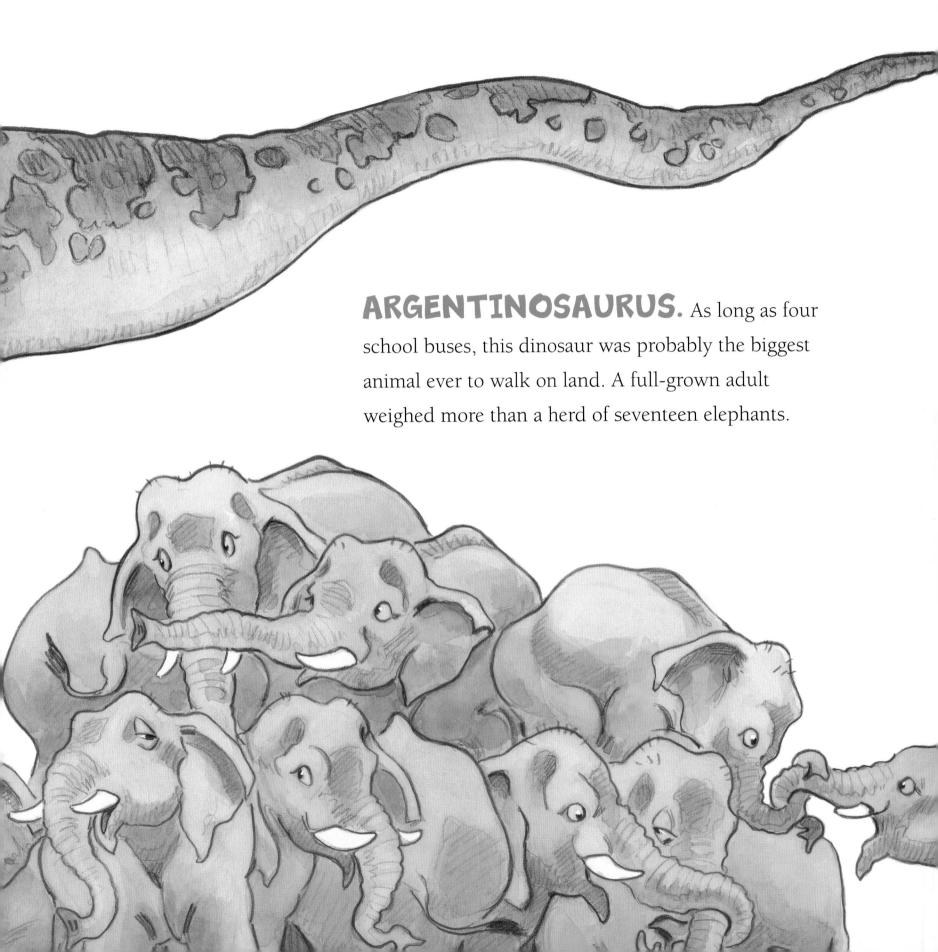

ARGENTINOSAURUS. As long as four school buses, this dinosaur was probably the biggest animal ever to walk on land. A full-grown adult weighed more than a herd of seventeen elephants.

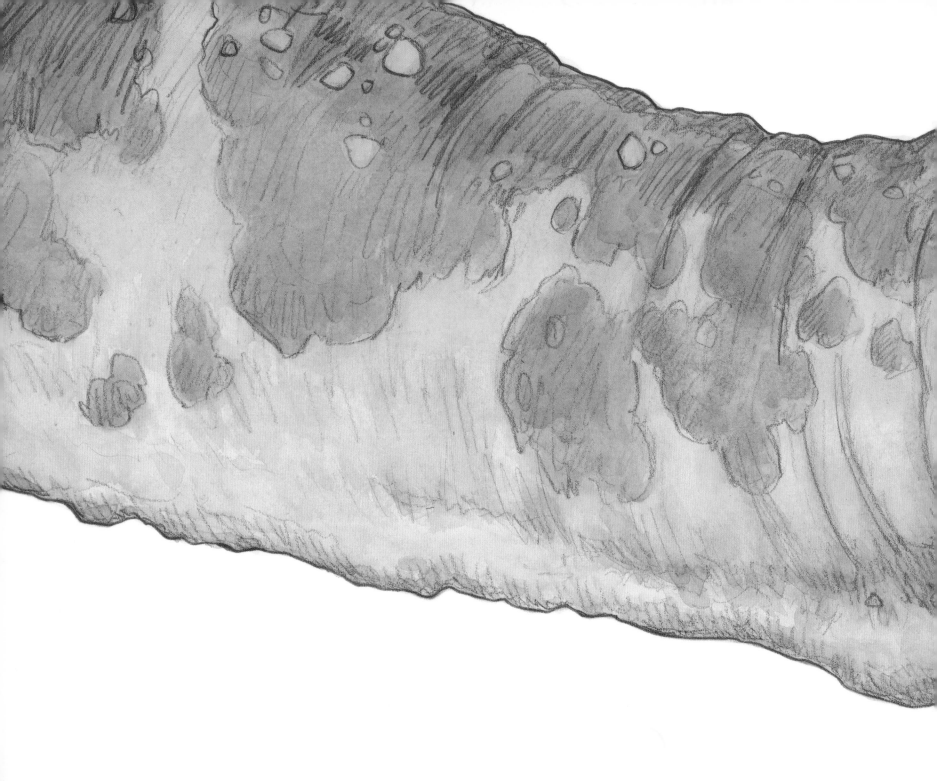

An *Argentinosaurus* was an incredible 45,000 times **BIGGER** than *Microraptor*. But the largest dinosaur was only dangerous if you were a tree. *Argentinosaurus* must have eaten them by the ton.

Dinosaurs really did come in every size—as small as birds,
or bigger than herds, and everything in between!

Tyrannosaurus rex (**tie-RAN-o-SORE-us rex**)
Up to 46 feet long, weighed perhaps 4.5–7 tons
Late Cretaceous (68–65 million years ago)

Argentinosaurus (**arh-gen-TEEN-o-SORE-us**)
Up to 130 feet long, weighed perhaps 80–100 tons
Middle Cretaceous (100–93 million years ago)

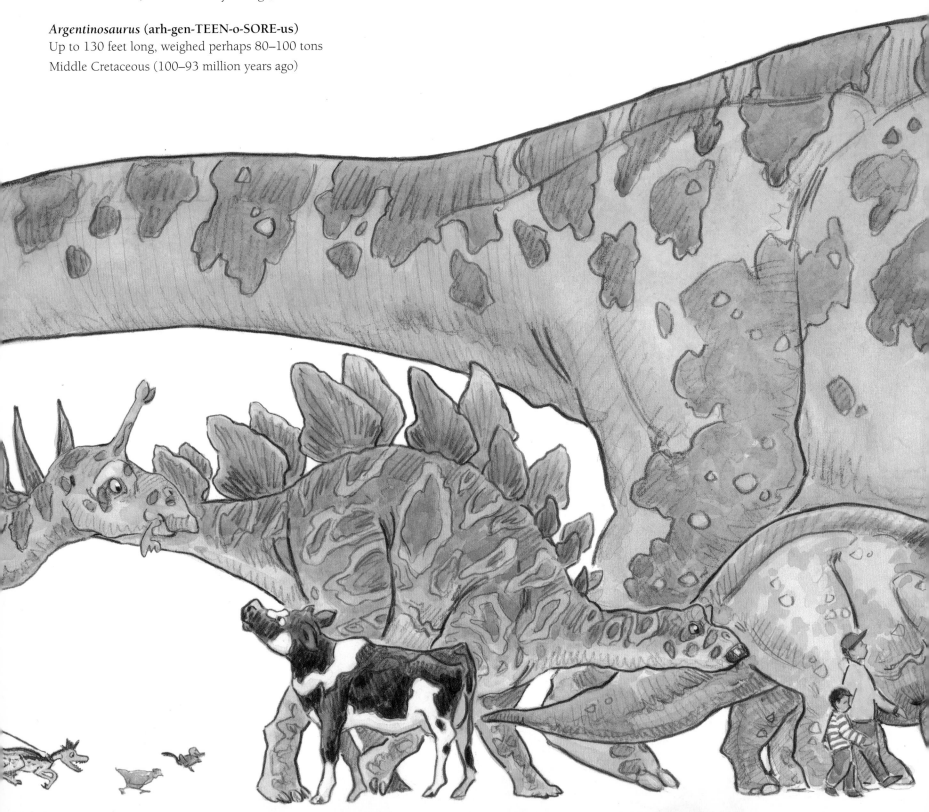

COMPARE THE SIZE OF EACH DINOSAUR

Microraptor (MIE-kro-RAP-tor)
1.5–2 feet long, probably weighed 2–4 pounds
Early Cretaceous (130–125 million years ago)

Protoceratops (pro-toe-SAIR-uh-tops)
Averaged 6.5 feet long, probably weighed 400–900 pounds
Late Cretaceous (86–71 million years ago)

Leaellynasaura (lee-ELL-in-ah-SORE-ah)
6.5 feet long, may have weighed up to 150 pounds
Early Cretaceous (112–99 million years ago)

Velociraptor (vel-O-si-RAP-tor)
5 to 6 feet long, probably weighed 15–33 pounds
Late Cretaceous (80–73 million years ago)

Stegosaurus (STEG-o-SORE-us)
Up to 30 feet long, weighed up to 2 tons
Late Jurassic (154–144 million years ago)

Tsintaosaurus (JING-dow-o-SORE-us)
Up to 33 feet long, probably weighed up to 3 tons
Late Cretaceous (80 million years ago)

Torosaurus (TORE-o-sore-us)
Up to 26 feet long, probably weighed up to 4–5 tons
Late Cretaceous (70–65 millions years ago)

Therizinosaurus (THER-i-ZEEN-o-SORE-us)
Up to 36 feet long, weighed up to 6 tons
Late Cretaceous (70–65 million years ago)

Struthiomimus (STRUTH-ee-o-MEEM-us)
Up to 11.5 feet long, weighed up to 650 pounds
Late Cretaceous (76–70 million years ago)

Ankylosaurus (an-KIE-loh-SORE-us)
33–36 feet long, weighed up to 4 tons
Late Cretaceous (68–65 million years ago)

HOW DO WE KNOW HOW BIG DINOSAURS WERE?

We can see how big dinosaurs were by looking at fossils of their bones. Sometimes when a dinosaur died, its body was buried quickly by sand or mud. Over millions of years, the mud and sand turned to solid rock. At the same time, water seeped in through the mud carrying minerals that slowly replaced the bone with rock and made a fossil.

Scientists uncover fossils in the ground. If they find enough fossils, they can put an entire dinosaur skeleton together. Then they work with artists to draw pictures and make models that show what the dinosaurs might have looked like.

If you can see how large a dinosaur skeleton is, you can imagine how this dinosaur compares to animals alive today. For example, *Velociraptor* had a lightweight body and probably weighed 15 to 33 pounds. That means it stood as tall, and weighed as much, as a medium-sized dog. But it had a much longer tail. The dinosaurs in this book are just a tiny portion of all the different species that once lived, but they show their wonderful variety and amazing extremes.

Microraptor and *Argentinosuarus* didn't live at the same time or in the same place, but it is interesting to compare these dinosaurs to get an idea of their range in size.

To determine the proportions of dinosaurs in this book, I used actual skeletal measurements taken from the books and websites listed below. I also visited the Royal Tyrrell Museum, the American Museum of Natural History, and the Museum of the Rockies. In some cases few fossils have been found, so there are only a couple of examples from which to draw conclusions. But with many species, scientists have found individuals ranging from juvenile to adult.

For further reading on dinosaur sizes and other facts:

WEBSITES

BBC Nature Prehistoric Life
bbc.co.uk/nature/prehistoric

Enchanted Learning Dinosaurs
enchantedlearning.com/subjects/dinosaurs

BOOKS

Barrett, P., and R. Martin. *National Geographic Dinosaurs*. Washington, D.C.: National Geographic Society, 2001.

Holtz, T. R., and V. Rey. *Dinosaurs: The Most Complete, Up-to-Date Encyclopedia for Dinosaur Lovers of All Ages*. New York: Random House Books for Young Readers, 2007.

Paul, G. S. *The Princeton Field Guide to Dinosaurs* (Princeton Field Guides). Princeton, NJ: Princeton University Press, 2010.

Copyright © 2013 by Lita Judge
Published by Roaring Brook Press, a division of Holtzbrinck Publishing Holdings
Limited Partnership
175 Fifth Avenue, New York, New York 10010
mackids.com
All rights reserved

Library of Congress Cataloging-in-Publication Data
Judge, Lita.
    How big were dinosaurs? / Lita Judge.
        pages   cm
    Summary: "Dinosaurs and modern life collide in a very young picture
  book that clearly illustrates how big dinosaurs really were"—Provided
  by publisher.
    ISBN 978-1-59643-719-7 (hardback)
    1. Dinosaurs—Size—Juvenile literature.   I. Title.

    QE861.5.J84 2013
    567.9—dc23

                                        2013001327

Roaring Brook Press books may be purchased for business or promotional use.
For information on bulk purchases please contact Macmillan Corporate and Premium Sales
Department at (800) 221-7945 x5442 or by email at specialmarkets@macmillan.com.

First edition 2013
Book design by Roberta Pressel
Printed in China by South China Printing Co. Ltd.,
Dongguan City, Guangdong Province

10   9   8   7   6   5   4   3   2   1